All the jokes in this book were collected from children around the country during Children's Book Week. Hundreds came in to the Macmillan offices every week and we all had a great time reading them and choosing the funniest ones; we'd like to thank all the contributors for sharing their jokes with us, and for raising money for Save the Children.

There are also a few jokes from published authors: can you spot their names in the Index?

The Daily Telegraph
CHILDREN'S BOOK WEEK
JOKE BOOK!

MACMILLAN CHILDREN'S BOOKS

CHILDREN'S BOOK WEEK

First published 1994 by
Macmillan Children's Books
Macmillan Publishers Limited
a division of Macmillan Publishers
Cavaye Place London SW10 9PG
and Basingstoke

Associated companies throughout the world

ISBN 0 330 33415 8

Collection copyright © The Save the Children Fund 1994
Registered Charity Number 213890

9 8 7 6 5 4 3

A CIP catalogue record for this book is available from the British
Library.

Designed by Anne Clue
Printed and bound in Great Britain by
Cox & Wyman Ltd, Reading, Berkshire

JOKE BOOK!

FOREWORD

....

What's black and white and yellow and blue and green and purple and orange and sky-blue pink and READ all over?

Young Telegraph that's what - The Daily Telegraph's colourful newspaper for children.

....

Young Telegraph is a fact-packed read on all your favourite subjects. It's fun-filled too with loads of jokes to keep you chuckling.

FOREWORD

The jokes you'll find in this book, however, have one thing in common: they all came from children who visited *The Daily Telegraph's* brilliant Book Bus. The profits from this rib-tickling tome will be helping children around the world because every book sold raises 22p for the Save the Children Fund. Hooray!

You'll find the Book Bus out and about during Children's Book Week. But you can find more great gags like these each and every week in *Young Telegraph*. And you'll

JOKE BOOK!

find *Young Telegraph* in *The Daily Telegraph* every Saturday – don't miss it!

Caroline Clayton
EDITOR, *Young Telegraph*

FOREWORD

Where do sheep have their hair cut?

At the baabaa's!

Where do you weigh whales?

At the whale way station!

Where would you see a prehistoric cow?

In a mooseum!

Where do cows go on holiday?

Moo York!

DOCTOR

Doctor, doctor, I feel like a snooker ball.

Well, get to the back of the queue then.

Doctor, doctor, I feel like a bee.

Well, give me a buzz if things get worse.

DOCTOR

Doctor, doctor, I feel like a pair of curtains.

Pull yourself together lad.

Doctor, doctor, my wife feels like a duck.

Bring her in then.

I can't, she's just flown south for the winter.

Doctor, doctor, the invisible man's just outside.

Well, tell him I can't see him without an appointment.

12

Doctor, doctor, I feel like a door bell.

Take these pills and then give me a ring.

Doctor, doctor, can you help me?
Yes, what's wrong?
Everyone keeps ignoring me.
Next!

Doctor, doctor, I feel like an ice-cream.

So do I, could you order two please!

Doctor, doctor, I feel like a pack of cards.

Sit down, and I'll deal with you in a minute.

Doctor, doctor, I feel flat.
What has come over you today?
Three cars and a bus.

13

Doctor, doctor, there's a nut in my ear.

That's all right, I'll put some chocolate in and it'll come out a treat!

Doctor, doctor, I feel like a piece of rope.

Calm down and stop getting yourself in a twist.

Doctor, doctor, nobody listens to me anymore.

Next!

Doctor, doctor, I keep thinking I'm a dog.

How long have you felt like this?

Ever since I was a puppy.

Doctor, doctor, I'm only four foot two.

Well, you'll just have to be a little patient.

Doctor, doctor, I feel like a toilet.

Yes, you look a bit flushed.

Doctor, doctor, can you help me out?

Certainly, which way did you come in?

Doctor, doctor, I think I've lost my memory.

How did that happen?

How did what happen?

WHY?

Why was 6 upset?

Because 7 8 9!

Why did the elephant paint his toenails red?

So he could hide in a cherry tree!

Why aren't 15 year olds allowed to vote?

Take That would be the next Prime Minister!

Why did the bakers go on strike?

They wanted more dough!

Why did the duck sink when he went for a swim?

Because it had a quack in it!

Why do birds fly south?

Because it's too far to walk!

Why do elephants paint the soles of their feet yellow?

So they can hide upside-down in bowls of custard!

But I've never seen an elephant in a bowl of custard.

That shows how good their disguise is!

WHY?

Why did the cockerel cross the road?

To show his girlfriend he wasn't chicken!

Why did the punk cross the road?

Because it was stapled to the chicken!

Why did the hedgehog cross the road?

To prove he had guts!

Why did the chewing-gum cross the road?

Because it was stuck to the chicken's foot!

....

Why did the dinosaur cross the road?

Because there weren't any chickens in those days!

(But there weren't any roads either . . .)

....

Why did the he cross the road?

Because it was looking for the n!

....

Why did the orange stop in the middle of the road?

Because it ran out of juice!

....

Why did the turtle cross the road?

Because the chicken was on holiday!

WHY?

Why did the chicken cross the road?

Because it saw a man laying bricks!

Why did the chicken cross the road?

To get to the other side!

Why did the hand cross the road?

To get to the second-hand shop!

Why did the hedgehog cross the road?

To see his flatmate!

20

Why did the boy take a pencil to bed?

So he would be able to draw the curtains!

Why are eggs like bricks?

They both have to be laid.

Why are fish easy to weigh?

Because they've got their own scales!

Why did the tomato blush?

Because he saw the salad dressing!

Why do cows wear cow bells?

Because their horns don't work!

WHY?

Why wouldn't Noah let the two maggots in the apple on to his ark?

Because he only took animals in pears!

Why do space aliens wear bullet-proof vests?

Because of shooting stars!

Why can't bananas sunbathe?

Because they peel!

Why did the robber have a bath before he robbed the bank?

He wanted a clean getaway!

JOKE BOOK!

Why are bananas never lonely?

Because they go around in bunches!

Why is cream more expensive than milk?

Because cows find it difficult to sit on small pots!

Why did the little boy take an orange to the leisure centre?

To play squash!

Why did the mushroom have so many friends?

Because he was a fungi (fun guy, geddit?)!

23

WHY?

Why didn't the crisps catch the bus?

Because they were Walkers!

Why are cooks so cruel?

Because they beat eggs, whip cream and batter fish!

Why did the bus stop?

Because he saw a zebra crossing!

Why did the boy take his tool-kit to bed with him?

So he could make his bed in the morning!

JOKE BOOK!

Why can't a clock see anything?

Because it always covers its face with its hands!

Why can't leopards escape from the zoo?

Because they always get spotted!

Why do seals lie on rocks?

If they lay under them they would be squashed!

Why can't an elephant go swimming with another elephant on top?

Because they've only got one pair of trunks between them!

WHY?

Why are flowers so lazy?
Because they spend all day in beds!

Why is a football pitch wet?
Because the footballers dribble!

Why did the teacher wear sunglasses?
Because she had a bright class!

Why don't polar bears eat penguins?
Because they can't get the wrappers off!

Why did the golfer have two pairs of trousers on?

In case he got a hole in one!

Why can't the Queen wave with this hand?

Because it's my hand!

Why did the bat miss the bus?

Because he hung around too long!

Why does a bear wear a fur coat?

Because he would look ridiculous in a mackintosh!

WHY?

Why can't you play cards in the jungle?

Because there are too many cheetahs!

Why did the skeleton run up the tree?

Because the dog was after his bones!

Why was the sand yellow?

Because the sea weed!

Why do bees fly with their legs crossed?

Because they are looking for B.P. stations!

....

Why did the parrot wear a raincoat?

Because he wanted to be Polly unsaturated!

....

Why did the boy throw the clock out of the window?

Because he wanted to see time fly!

....

Why can't a car play football?

Because it only has one boot!

....

Why did the frying pan fancy the bowl?

Because he was a dish!

....

Why does the sea roar?

Well, wouldn't you roar if you had crabs on your bottom?

....

Why does an elephant wear sneakers?

So he can sneak up on mice!

....

Why were the flies playing football on a saucer?

They were playing for the cup.

....

Why did the prune go out with a sultana?

Because he couldn't find a date!

Why did the ship tremble at the bottom of the sea?

Because it was a nervous wreck!

Why are elephants so wrinkled?

Have you ever tried ironing one?

Why do storks lift one leg?

Because if they lifted both they'd fall over.

Limericks

I once had a parrot called Polly
Who flew down and bit my ice lolly
It broke it's beak
Now it can't speak
So no more lolly for Polly!

A fellow I know, name of Tom
Manufactured his own atom bomb
It went off by surprise
And I'm not telling lies
That was the end of old Tom

There was once a builder called Bob
Who was a bit of a hog
For lunch he had cake
For tea he had steak
That greedy old man called Bob

There once was an old hamster named Larry
Who decided he was going to marry
So he changed his life
And looked for a wife
And that was the end of old Larry

JOKE BOOK!

There once was a teacher named Pat
Who was exceedingly fat
She tripped on a stair -
Now I don't dare
Tell you how she went splat!

There once was a young man named Stan
Who drove a very old van
With a splutter and a cough
The wheels fell off
And that was the end of Stan's van

There once was a pony called Jake
Who, sadly, was thin as a rake
He ignored his dinner
And got thinner and thinner
And that was the end of poor Jake

There once was a young lady from Spain
And she liked to travel by plane
But a terrible thing happened
On the plane to Manhatten
They flew straight into a crane

Limericks

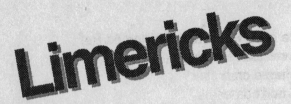

There once was a very strong cat
Who had a fight with a bat
The bat flew away
And at the end of the day
The cat had a scrap with a rat

There was an old man called Jake
Who had a poisonous snake
It bit his head
And now he's dead
So that was the end of Jake

There once was an old billy goat
With a ballbearing stuck in his throat
He coughed and he spluttered
And in anguish he muttered
From now on I'll just stick to oats

There once was a snake named Drake
Who started a fight with a rake
It cut off his tail
Drake went very pale
And that is the end of my tale

There once was a rabbit called Buster
Who I mistook for a feather duster
I polished a chair
And now I don't dare
To tell you what happened to Buster

There once was a pony called Matt
Who was exceedingly fat
With a tumble and a sneeze
He fell on his knees
And that was the end of poor Matt

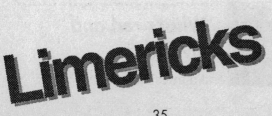

Limericks

WHAT'S . . .

....

What's black and white and acts like a horse?

A zebra

....

What's yellow and dangerous?

Shark-infested custard.

....

What's green and furry on top and yellow underneath?

Last week's custard.

....

What's red and invisible?

An invisible tomato!

36

JOKE BOOK!

What's green and hairy and goes up and down?

A gooseberry in a lift.

What's green and noisy and goes up and down?

A gooseberry blowing raspberries in a lift!

What's black and white, black and white, black and white?

A penguin rolling down a hill.

What's grey and has a trunk?

A mouse going on holiday.

WHAT?

37

What's green and round and goes camping?

A Brussel Scout.

What's black and white and dotted red all over?

A zebra with chicken pox.

What's big, grey and has 16 wheels?

An elephant on roller-skates.

What's yellow and white and gets eaten at 100mph?

A train driver's egg sandwich.

JOKE BOOK!

What's green with red spots?

A frog with measles.

What's yellow and stupid?

Thick custard.

What's red and goes ho ho plop?

Father Christmas laughing his head off.

What's big, red and eats rocks?

A big, red rock eater.

What's a hedgehog's favourite meal?

Prickled onions.

What's the wettest animal in the world?

A rain-deer.

What's tall and smells nice?

A Giraffe-adil.

What's a dog when it's hot?

A hot-dog.

What's a crocodile's favourite game?

Snap.

What's green, slimy, ugly and has 1,000 legs?

I don't know.

I don't know either, but there's one crawling up your back!

What's a frog's favourite flower?

A crocus.

What's the opposite to cock-a-doodle-doo?

Cock-a-doodle-don't!

What's Dracula's favourite drink?

Fangta.

What's an Australian's favourite drink?

Coca Koala.

What's the opposite of right?

Left.

Wrong - it's wrong.

42

JOKE BOOK!

What's the most common phrase at school?

I don't know!

What's white when it's dirty?

A black-board.

What's an ig?

An eskimo house without a loo.

What's a horse's favourite game?

Stable tennis.

WHAT?

What's the worst vegetable to have on a ship?

A leek.

What's the fastest cake in the world?

Scone. (Say it very fast.)

What's a thousand feet high and wobbles?

The Trifle Tower.

What's a cow's favourite vegetable?

A cowat.

JOKE BOOK!

What's the difference between a penguin and an elephant?

You can eat a p - p - p - Penguin!

What's the difference between a fish and a piano?

You can't tuna fish!

What's the difference between a fireman and a soldier?

You can't dip a fireman in your boiled egg!

What's got a head and a tail but no body?

A coin!

What's the most important thing you can take into the desert?

A thirst-aid kit.

What's a grasshopper?

An insect on a pogo-stick.

What's a skeleton's favourite instrument?

A trom-bone.

WHAT . . .

What did the giant
canary say?

CHIRP!!!

What do you give an
elephant with big
feet?

Lots of room.

What does a lion
have for breakfast?

Cheetabix.

What does a
Frenchman have for
breakfast?

Huit-heure-bix.

47

CHILDREN'S BOOK WEEK

What happens if you go to sleep with your head under the pillow?

The fairies take out all your teeth!

What goes ninety-nine clonk, ninety-nine clonk?

A centipede with a wooden leg

What will they call Postman Pat when he retires?

Pat

What do jelly babies wear on their feet?

Gumboots.

What did the giant mouse say?

EEEE...K!

What gets wetter as it dries?

A towel!

What does Tarzan sing at Christmas?

Jungle bells, jungle bells, jungle all the way!

What do sea monsters eat?

Fish and ships.

What jumps up and down in front of a car?

Froglights.

What do you do with a rubber trumpet?

Join an elastic band.

What do sheep shout at football matches?

'Ere ewe go! 'Ere ewe go! 'Ere ewe go!

What kind of cows live in the far north?

Eskimoos.

JOKE BOOK!

What begins with a T, ends with a T and has T in it?

A teapot.

What do frogs drink?

Croak-a-cola.

What was the tortoise doing on the motorway?

About 150 milimetres an hour.

What does a goose eat?

Gooseberries.

51

What do cats eat for breakfast?

Mice crispies.

What goes over the water, under the water, on the water and yet never touches the water?

An egg in a duck's tummy!

What goes out brown and comes back white?

A teddy bear in a snow storm.

What did the postman deliver to Dracula?

Fang mail.

What American city has lots of cows?

Moo York.

What bird is always out of breath?

A puffin.

What do you do if you see a spaceman?

Park in it, man!

What did the frog use to cross the road?

The green cross toad.

What bird spends most of its time on its knees?

A bird of prey.

What burglar burgles meat?

A hamburglar.

What do cars do at discos?

A brake dance.

What do you serve, but never eat?

A tennis ball.

What do you give a sick pig?

Oinkment.

What do you give a sick bird?

Tweetment.

What do you give an injured lemon?

Lemon aid.

What lives in a field and has 4,000 legs?

Grass - I was lying about the legs!

WHAT?

What goes straight up in the air and wobbles?

A jellycopter.

What did the spaceman see in his frying pan?

An unidentified frying object.

What happened when the bull went into the china shop?

He had a smashing time.

What do you do if you find a blue banana?

Try to cheer it up.

JOKE BOOK!

What sort of stone can you eat?

Rock.

What crisps fly?

Plain ones.

What coat burns?

A blazer.

What do hedgehogs have for breakfast?

Prickled onions.

What were Tarzan's last words?

'Who greased the vine?'

WHAT?

WHAT DID THE . . . SAY TO THE . . .

....

What did the big chimney say to the little chimney?

You're too young to smoke.

....

What did the big bottle say to the little bottle?

You're too young to get drunk!

....

What did the big telephone say to the little telephone?

You're too young to get engaged.

JOKE BOOK!

What did the big traffic light say to the little traffic light?

Don't look - I'm changing

What did the baby hedgehog say to the cactus?

Is that you, mum?

What did the big piece of dough say to the little piece of dough?

You'll still be kneaded!

What did the sea say to the sand?

Nothing, he just waved.

What did the grape say when the elephant sat on him?

Nothing, he just gave out a little wine.

What did the frog say when he saw all the books in the library?

Read it! Read it! Read it!

What did the cookie say to the biscuit?

Oh, crumbs!

What did the cannibal say when he couldn't eat any more?

I couldn't eat another mortal.

What did the man say when his watch fell out of the window?

How time flies!

What did one wall say to the other wall?

I'll meet you at the corner.

What did the hungry donkey say when it only had thistles to eat?

Thistle have to do .

What does a Spanish farmer say to his hens?

Olé!

CHILDREN'S BOOK WEEK

What did one pencil say to the other?

I've got a terrible leadache.

What did the policeman say to his tummy?

You're under a vest.

What did the cannibal say to the explorer?

Nice to meat you!

WHAT DO YOU GET . . .

....

What do you get if you cross a chicken with gunpowder?

An egg-splosion.

....

What do you get if you cross two elephants and a fish?

Swimming trunks.

....

What do you get if you cross a Tyrannosaurus Rex and a snowman?

Frostbite!

WHAT?

WHAT?

What do you get if you phone 666?

An upside-down police car.

What do you get if you cross a kangaroo and a sheep?

A woolly jumper with huge pockets.

What do you get if you cross a stereo with a refridgerator?

Cool music.

What do you get if you cross a hedgehog with a giraffe?

A giant toothbrush.

What do you get if you cross a gorilla?

A black eye.

What do you get if you cross an elephant with a fish?

Swimming trunks.

What do you get if you cross a cow, a sheep and a goat?

A milky-baa kid.

What do you get if you cross an elephant with a hose?

A jumbo jet.

WHAT?

What do you get if you cross a kangaroo with a hippopotamus?

Flat Australians.

What do you get if you cross a teddy bear with a pig?

A teddy boar.

What do you get if you cross a centipede with a parrot?

A walkie-talkie.

What do you get if you cross a hen with a dog?

Pooched eggs.

JOKE BOOK!

··

What do you get if a sheep walks under a rain cloud?

A sheep who is under the weather.

··

What do you get when you plant a gun in the garden?

Lots of little shoots.

··

What do you get if you pour boiling water down a rabbit hole?

A hot cross bunny.

WHAT?

What do you get if there is a queue outside the barber's shop?

A barbercue.

What do you get if you drop a piano on a soldier?

A flat major.

WHAT DO YOU CALL . . .

What do you call a chicken in a shellsuit?

An egg.

What do you call a Skoda at the top of a hill?

A miracle!

What do you call a Skoda with a sunroof?

A skip.

What do you call a fish with no eyes?

Fsh.

What do you call a house with pink bricks?

A pink house.

What do you call a house with blue bricks?

A blue house.

What do you call a house with green bricks?

A green house.

No, a greenhouse is made of glass!

JOKE BOOK!

What do you call a dog with no ears?

Anything - he still won't come.

What do you call a deer with no eyes?

No idea!

What do you call a bear with no hair?

Fred bear.

What do you call a one-eyed dinosaur?

Doyouthinkhesawus?

What do you call a one-eyed dinosaur's dog?

Doyouthinkhesawus Rex.

WHAT?

What do you call a dinosaur who can't walk properly?

A Staggersaurus.

What do you call a gorilla with bananas in his ears?

Anything you like - he can't hear you!

What do you call two robbers?

A pair of knickers!

What do you call a camel with 3 humps?

Humphrey.

JOKE BOOK!

What do you call a
man with a spade on
his head?

Doug.

What do you call a
man without a spade
on his head?

Douglas.

What do you call a
man with a car on his
head?

Jack.

What do you call a
man with a seagull on
his head?

Cliff.

What do you call a man with a wooden head?

Edward.

What do you call a man with two wooden heads?

Edward Wood.

What do you call a man with three wooden heads?

Edward Woodward.

What do you call a man with four wooden heads?

I don't know, but Edward Woodward would.

What do you call a woman who plays snooker with a pint of beer on her head?

Beer Tricks Potter.

What do you call a girl with a frog on her head?

Lily.

What do you call a sleeping bull?

A bull dozer.

What do you call a sheep with no legs?

A cloud.

What do you call a snowman with a suntan?

A puddle.

What do you call a smelly bear?

Winnie-the-Pooh.

What do you call an apple when it's cross?

Apple Grumble.

What do you call an ant with frogs' legs?

Ant-thibian.

....

What do you call a woodpecker with no beak?

A headbanger.

Knock knock
Who's there?
Gran
Gran who?
Knock knock
Who's there?
Gran
Gran who?
Knock knock
Who's there?
Gran
Gran who?
Knock knock
Who's there?
Aunt
Aunt who?
Aunt you glad I'm not another Gran!

Knock knock
Who's there?
Pudding
Pudding who?
Pudding on your shoes before your trousers is a bad idea!

Knock knock
Who's there?
Tina
Tina who?
Tina Tomatoes!

Knock knock
Who's there?
Nicholas
Nicholas who?
Nicholas ladies shouldn't climb trees!

Knock knock
Who's there?
Anna
Anna who?
Anna-pple just fell on my head!

Knock knock
Who's there?
Mandy
Mandy who?
Mandy lifeboat the ship's sinking!

Knock knock
Who's there?
Owl
Owl who?
Owl do you if you don't open the door!

JOKE BOOK!

Knock knock
Who's there?
Doctor
Doctor who?
I am Doctor Who!

Knock knock
Who's there?
Scott
Scott who?
Scott nothing to do with you!

Knock knock
Who's there?
Wendy
Wendy who?
Wendy saints go marching in!

Knock knock
Who's there?
Lettuce
Lettuce who?
Lettuce in quick!

Knock knock
Who's there?
Isabel
Isabel who?
Isabel necessary on a bicycle?

Knock knock
Who's there?
Egburt
Egburt who?
Egburt no bacon!

Knock knock
Who's there?
Fish
Fish who?
Bless you!

Knock knock
Who's there?
Furry
Furry who?
Furry's a jolly good fellow!

Knock knock
Who's there?
Watson
Watson who?
Nothing much. What's new with you?

Knock knock
Who's there?
Felix
Felix who?
Felix my ice-cream, I'll lick his!

Knock knock
Who's there?
Phil
Phil who?
Phil us a glass of water please!

Knock knock
Who's there?
Small man
Small man who?
Small man who can't reach the doorbell!

Knock knock
Who's there?
Albert
Albert who?
Albert you'll never guess!

Knock knock
Who's there?
Will
Will who?
Will you mind your own business?

Knock knock
Who's there?
Zippy
Zippy who?
Zippedy doo dah, zippedy day, my oh my what a wonderful day!

Knock knock
Who's there?
Boo
Boo who?
There's no need to cry!

Knock knock
Who's there?
Alick
Alick who?
A lick my lollipop, you lick yours!

Knock knock
Who's there?
Me
Me who?
I never knew you had a cat!

Knock knock
Who's there?
Howie
Howie who?
**I'm fine thanks,
how are you?**

Knock knock
Who's there?
Ivor
Ivor who?
**Ivor got a lovely bunch of
coconuts, see them all a standing
in a row . . .**

HOW?

How do you make gold soup?
Put nine carrots in it!

How do you make a jacket last?
Make the trousers first!

How do you make a swiss roll?
Push him down a hill!

How do you hire a horse?
Buy it two pairs of stilts!

How does an eskimo stop his teeth from freezing?
He grits them!

How do you start a teddy race?

Ready, Teddy, GO!

How do you make a Mexican chilli?

Take him to the North Pole!

How do you make a band stand?

Hide all their chairs!

How did the dinosaurs know we were coming?

Because the Bronto-saw-us!

How do you get a dinosaur to fly?

Buy it an airline ticket!

HOW?

CHILDREN'S BOOK WEEK

HOW?

How do we know Pyrex dishes come from Cornwall?

Ever heard of The Pyrex of Penzance?

How do you get rid of a boomerang?

Throw it down a one way street!

How does a skeleton ring up his friends?

On a telebone!

How do you get a baby to go to sleep on the moon?

Rocket!

··

How do you get a pat on the head?

Sit under a cow!

··

How do you keep cool at a football match?

Stand next to a fan!

··

How can you tell if there's an elephant in the fridge?

There are footprints in the butter!

··

How did the skeleton get in the house?

With a skeleton key!

HOW?

Did you hear the one about the...

Forty sheep went through a gap.
Forty more after that.
Then a dog.
Then a man.
How many feet was that?
(Answer: Two.)

'So you say your school's been burgled',
the policeman scratched his face . . .
'Mmm, and you've nothing left to write with.
Yes, this looks like a pencil case.'

A cabbage, a bean and a tomato had a race.
This is what happened. The bean was in the
lead, the cabbage was second and the tomato
tried to ketchup.

When is the best time to buy a canary?
When it's going cheap.

JOKE BOOK!

There was a man who went into a pet shop and said, 'Can I have a wasp please?' The shop assistant said they did not sell wasps. The man said 'But there is one in the window!'

Two owls playing pool,
One said 'Two hits!'
The other said
'Two hits to who!?'

Did you hear about the fight in the biscuit tin? The Bandit hit the Yo Yo and got away in a Taxi!

A cowboy went into town on Monday, stayed Tuesday and Wednesday and Thursday and came home the following day on Tuesday. How did he do that?
(Answer: His horse was called Tuesday.)

Are you a light sleeper?
No, I sleep in the dark.

Did you hear the one about the...

Did you hear the one about the...

A man was in the park and he saw a penguin. He showed it to a nearby policeman. He was told to take it to the zoo. The next day the policeman saw him again with the penguin and asked him why. The man said,
'He enjoyed the zoo so much, I'm taking him to the pictures today!'

A barrel of beer fell on a man but he wasn't hurt. Why not?
(Answer: Because it was light ale.)

'My new horse is very well-mannered.'
'That's nice.'
'Yes, isn't it? Every time we come to a jump he stops and lets me get off first!'

Two crisps were crossing the street, when a man pulled up in a car and asked them if they would like a lift.
'Oh no,' they said, 'We're Walkers!'

A Scottish man goes to stay with a Canadian friend. When he gets there they take him to his lodge. On the wall he sees a huge head and asks what it is. His friend says it's a moose so the Scottish man says,
'If that's a mouse, what on earth do your cats look like!?'

Three men were walking along the beach one day when they see a cave. The first man goes in first and is just eyeing up a banknote lying on a big rock when a ghostly voice calls out:
'I am the ghost of Auntie Mabel and
this five pounds stays on the table!'
The second man goes in and is reaching for the note when the same thing happens again. The third man goes in, sees the five pounds and cries out,
'I am the ghost of Davy Crockett
and this five pounds goes in my pocket!'

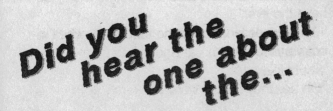
Did you hear the one about the...

Did you hear the one about the...

Tropical Parrots by Prit E Polley

Jumping off the Cliff by Countme Owt

Long Walk by Miss D Bus

There were 3 men, and they went hunting. They caught a deer and cooked it, but none of them knew which parts of the deer to eat. The first man suggested they decide according to which football team they each supported.

'I support Hearts,' he said, 'So I'll eat the heart.'

'I support Liverpool,' said the second man, 'So I'll have the liver.'

'I support Arsenal,' said the third man, 'But I'm not very hungry . . .'

JOKE BOOK!

There was a new boy in the class. The teacher said 'What's your name?'
'Jason Mickey Smith.' replied the boy.
I'll just call you Jason Smith, I think.' said the teacher.
'My father wouldn't like that,' said Jason, 'He doesn't like people taking the Mickey out of my name!'

A burglar was burgling a house when he heard a voice behind him saying,
'Jesus is watching you!' so he shone his torch around the room and saw a parrot. 'What's your name?' he asked it. 'Roosevelt.' replied the parrot.
'That's a funny name for a parrot.'
'Well - Jesus is a funny name for the Rottweiler that's standing behind you!'

Have you heard the one about the bed?
It hasn't been made yet!

Did you hear the one about the...

Did you hear the one about the...

Waiter, waiter, have you got chicken legs?
No, I always walk like this!

Son: Dad, can I get married?
Dad: Yes, who to?
Son: Granny.
Dad: You can't marry my mother.
Son: Why not? You married mine!

'Mum! I can't get to sleep!'
'Well, sleep on the end of the bed and you will soon drop off!'

A teacher tells his class to draw a picture of their own choice. One boy draws a picture of an aeroplane with four people in it. The teacher asks who they are and the boy replies, 'Well, in the back there is Jesus, Mary and Joseph.'
'And who is in the front?' asks the teacher.
'Pontius Pilate, of course!'

There were three pieces of string. One piece of string goes into a pub and asks for a drink. The barman asks, 'Are you a piece of string?'
'Yes.'
'Sorry, we don't serve pieces of string.'
The second piece of string goes into the pub and the same thing happens, so the third piece of string goes confidently into the bar and asks for a drink.
'Are you a piece of string?'
'No, I'm a frayed knot!'

Peter and Tim were on a cliff top. Tim got one budgie and put it under his arm and then got another budgie and put it under the other arm. He then jumped off the cliff. Peter ran down and said, 'Are you okay?', and Tim said, 'No, I've got things broken all over the place: I'm never doing this budgie jumping again!'

Did you hear the one about the...

Did you hear the one about the...

I was driving along when I hit a hare. I stopped, and luckily the car behind stopped and the driver was a vet.
'Can you do anything for him?' I asked.
'Yes,' he said, getting a bottle from his bag and giving the hare a few drops of liquid. In a matter of seconds the hare jumped up and ran away, stopping every now and again turning around, looking at the vet, and lifting his front paw.
'What did you give him?' I asked, amazed.
'Hair Restorer with a Permanent Wave!' he said.

'Have you seen a policeman around here?'
'No.'
'Do you know where the nearest police station is?'
'No.'
'Right then - stick 'em up!'

Which fly makes films?
Steven Spielbug.

JOKE BOOK!

There were three men - one from China, two from France. They all boarded a Jumbo to America, but there was just one problem: on the way there, the Jumbo went over France and the Frenchman waved and cried,
"Bye France!' The Chinese man was jealous and cried out, as he threw his cup and saucer out of the window, "Bye China!'

It all started in a zoo, in the lions' cages. The lions always had everyone else's leftovers for dinner. One day there was an accident in the fishtanks and all the fish died, and the keeper said, 'Oh! I'll give the fish to the lions!' and did. They gobbled them up. The next day there was an accident in the chimps' cage with the same result: chimp for dinner. The next day, there was an accident in the beehive and all the bees died. The keeper gave them to the lions for dinner. The next day a new lion arrived and asked the other lions what they got to eat.
'Well, this week we've had fish, chimps and mushy bees!'

Did you hear the one about the...

CHILDREN'S BOOK WEEK

Did you hear the one about the...

There were three old ladies walking down the road.
'It's windy, isn't it?' said the first.
'I thought it was Thursday?' said the second, and the third replied,
'I'm thirsty too, let's go and have a cup of tea.'

Customer	How much will it cost to take me to the station?
Cabby:	A fiver.
Customer:	How much for my suitcase?
Cabby:	No charge.
Customer:	OK, you take my suitcase, and I'll walk.

Imagine you're a bus driver. Five people are on the bus, two get off, seventeen get on, four get off, six come on and two get off. What's the bus driver's name?
(Answer: your name)

JOKE BOOK!

There were three men on an iceberg. Luckily one had a telescope. Suddenly he slipped it into his pocket and said 'Ship ahoy! We're saved! Here comes the Titanic!'

The three bears came downstairs for breakfast.
'Who's been eating my porridge?' growled Father Bear, looking at his empty bowl.
'Who's been eating my porridge?' squeaked Baby Bear, looking at his empty bowl.
'Shut up, you two,' said Mother Bear. 'I haven't had time to make it yet!'

A little boy was walking by an allotment. A man was pulling up some rhubarb which was over six feet high.
'Excuse me, sir. What do you put on your rhubarb?'
'Manure.'
'That's funny. My mum puts custard on mine!'

Did you hear the one about the...

Did you hear the one about the...

A man went into a butcher's shop and asked for a pound of bacon.
'Lean back?'
The man fell over and hit his head.

A little girl goes to school for the first time and her mum tells her not to do any handstands or cartwheels in the playground, or the boys will see her knickers.
She comes home that afternoon and her mum asked if the boys had seen her knickers.
'No,' she said, 'I took them off first.'

A man goes into Casualty with an injured arm. The doctor examines him and says he's broken it. The man asks,
'Will I be able to play the piano?'
'Yes,' replies the doctor.
'That's funny,' says the man, 'I couldn't play it before!'

JOKE BOOK!

One day a man escaped from jail. The police tracked him down about two weeks later. They were just about to put him in the police car, when the man said, 'Can I have one last song before my freedom is taken away from me?'
So he sang '300,000,000 green bottles standing on the wall!'

Sheila: I bet I know where you got your tie.
Eric: Go on then, smartie pants. Where?
Sheila: Round your neck!
Eric: Ha, ha, very funny. By the way, did you hear? All the trains had to stop today.
Sheila: No, why? Was there a strike?
Eric: No - they had to let the passengers off!
Sheila: I cried when I went to see that film last week.
Eric: Why, was it sad?
Sheila: Dunno - I never got in!

Did you hear the one about the...

Did you hear the one about the...

Two biscuits were rolling across the road.
One got run over.
What did the other one say?
CRUMBS!

Which sweet is the cleverest?
A smartie!

If everyone let bygones be bygones there
wouldn't be any history!

There were three men in a doctor's waiting
room. When the doctor came in, one started
reaching his hand up in the air, then rubbing one
hand against the other. The doctor asked him
what he was doing and he replied, 'Polishing the
stars.' The second man then did the same and
gave the doctor the same answer. The third man
then started walking his fingers across the floor.
When the doctor asked him what he was doing,
he replied, 'Running away from those two daft
loonies!'

I say, I say! My dog's got no nose!
How does he smell?
Terrible!

Have you got holes in your socks?
No.
Then how do you get them on?

My pen has run out.
Why don't you run after it then?

A man is lying in hospital after an accident, and the doctor comes up and says, 'I've got good news and bad news for you. The bad news is that we've got to cut off your legs, but the good news is that the man in the next door bed wants to buy your slippers!'

Did you hear the one about the...

Did you hear the one about the...

This boy goes round to ask his girlfriend's father if he can marry her. Her father opens the door and the boy says, 'Please sir, can I have your daughter's hand in marriage?'
'Sorry mate, but you'll have to have all of her if you're going to marry her!'

Sandra and Simon were arguing furiously over breakfast.
'Oh, you're stupid!' shouted Simon.
'Simon!' said their father, 'That's quite enough of that! Now, say you're sorry.'
'All right,' said Simon, 'Sandra, I'm sorry you're stupid.'

There were two men standing by the road. The first man said, 'Why on earth have you got a cauliflower on a lead?'
The second man said, 'But the man in the pet shop said it was a caulidog!'

Donald was standing at the top of an escalator, looking at the handrail.
'Are you all right, little boy?' asked a kind lady.
'Sure,' replied Donald. 'I'm just waiting for my chewing gum to come around again.'

Dad:　　Percy, did you get a good place in your exams?

Percy:　　Yes, Dad, right next to the radiator!

Did you hear about the fight in the fish shop?
The fish got battered!

There were three men, and they were each granted one wish as they went down a slide. The first man shouted 'BEER!' and he landed at the bottom in a pool of beer. The second man shouted 'MONEY!' and he landed in a pile of gold. The third man went whizzing down the slide shouting 'WHEEEE!' and he landed in it.

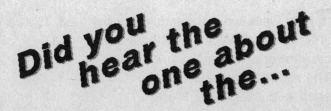

Did you hear the one about the...

Did you hear the one about the...

Did you know that Davy Crockett had three ears?
A left ear, a right ear and a wild frontier!

Do robots have brothers?
No, only transistors.

Did you hear the one about the boy who wanted a day off school?
He rang up his teacher to tell her that he'd lost his voice!

JOKE BOOK!

INDEX
of contributors

111

CHILDREN'S BOOK WEEK

INDEX

of contributors

Rachel Asprey
Mathew Atkinson

A

Lynne Abson
Rebecca Adams
Elizabeth Adams
Kristine Akid
Jenny Algar
Faye Allen
Nicholas Allen
Michelle Anderson
Matuzniy Anastazia
V Andrews
Michael Argent
Edward Armah
Alison Ashley
Louise Ashley
Rachel Ashmore

B

Sarah Bacon
Andrew Bailey
Gary Bailey
Marie Baker
Lucy Ballard
Emma Banks
Laura Barnett
Jamie Barrell
Lorraine Barwick
Catherine Bater
Kerry Beaumont
Jannat Begum
Sam Bendall

JOKE BOOK!

Sophie Beney
Craig Bennett
Gary Beresford
Candy Berry
Elinor Birch
Sam Bird
Debbie Blackledge
Laura Jane
Blenkinsop
Lucy Blown
Michelle Blown
James Blythe
Emma Borland
Sarah Borland
Rachel Bottomore
Nia Boulton
Tina Bradley
Kelly Bray
Beth Bridge
Michelle Bridges

Christopher Brown
James Brown
Louise Brown
Richard Brown
Gareth Bryant
Clare Buckham
Arzoo Buksh
Lucy Bumford
Kirsty Burgess
Matthew Burley
Jamie Burrell
Kate Burslem

C

Raeanne Cardwell
Gemma Carney
Tara Carpenter
Julie Carter

INDEX

CHILDREN'S BOOK WEEK

INDEX
of contributors

Deanna Casey
Tom Cash
Craig Catton
Gemma Chalmers
Richard Chandler
Keyleigh Jane
  Chapman
Julia Charnock
Aimee Clark
Charles Clark
Gary Clark
Marcia Clark
Sarah Clift
Michelle Coe
Liam Colclough
Thomas Colclough
Lauren Cold
Lucy Colter
Sarah Colquhoun

Tanya Cook
Lee Cooper
Claire Coupe
Sarah Court
Jonathan Cox
Craig
Catherine Crockett
Lyndsey Crook
Nicola Cumming
Rosemary
Cunningham

D

Hilary Dalton
Rebecca Dalwood
Daniel
Sian Davies

JOKE BOOK!

Amanda Davis
Sam Deakin
Louise Dickens
Sally Diver
M Dixon
Stephen Dobbs
Marc Donlevy
Joel Donnelly
Charlotte Dowd
Joanne Drabble
Elixabeth Ducar
Matthew Dudley
Eliza Dunlop
Ben Dunn
Joanne Dyer

Joanne Elliot
Charmaine Ellis
Richard Ellis
Philip John English
Ian Evans

E

Terence Eastburn
Sarah Eatough

F

Lee Farrow
Nicola Fellows
Sally Ferguson
Gareth Ferre
Ian Ferris
Anne Fine
John Fitt
Tom Flemming
Helen Foley
Michael Foley
Nathan Ford

INDEX
of contributors

Catherine Fortune
Alan Francis
Sarah Franks

G

Jacob Gadsby
Helen Gardiner
Donna Gatehouse
Koly Leigh George
Daniel Gilbert
Jemma Gill
Joanne Gill
Michelle Gillespie
Brough Girling
Alan Golding
Laura Good
Mark Gooding
Lisa Grainger

Benjamin Grandey
Eleanor Gratton
Robert Gray
Anna Green
Ruth Green
Ryan Green
Mary Jo Greenwood
Robert Grounds

H

Marie H
Robert Hallam
David Hardwick
Claire Hardy
Barney Harker
Sarah Harris
Jennifer Harrison
Sarah Harrison

JOKE BOOK!

Leanne Hart
Michelle Hart
Suzanne Harvey
Amanda Haslam
Jimmy Henderson
Clive Hennesy
Jack Herlitty
Rebbeca Heron
Christopher Herring
Amy Hickson
Laura High
Jonathan Hiles
Laura Hill
Harry Hills
Joanne Hobson
Lindsey Hodges
Sonny Hodges
Paul Hodson
Becky Holland
Dale Hollingworth

Louise Hosie
Laura Hoskins
Sarah Hoslam
Charlotte Hosler
Hannah Houchin
Rachel Howarth
Lianne Hudson
Martin Hughes
Hayley Hunt
Andrew Hunter
Rachel Angela
Hunter
Jimmy Huntley
William Hutchinson
Andrew Hutton
Christopher Hutton

I

Simon Ingledew

117

INDEX

of contributors

J

Jennifer
Jonathan
Andrew J
Cathy Jones
Nicola Jones
Richard Jones
Robert Jones
Andrew Johnson
Claire Johnson
Donna Johnstone
Victoria Jowett

K

Tara Kane

Naroup Kaur
Sam J Kelly
Jonathan Kerley
Victoria Kerridge
Sopie Kershaw
Stuart King
Laura Knott
Rachel Kozlowski
Stephen Kozlowski
Anitha Krishnan
Claire Kruman
Nicola Kurr

L

Liam
Lindsay
Debbie Lannen

JOKE BOOK!

Vicki Lannen
James Larkin
Helena Leake
Katie Lee
Rebecca Lee
Eloise Legelli
Rachel Levinson
Diana Lewis
Shelley Lewis
Sharna Lightly
Mark Linnard
William Linnard
Ciaran Lofts
Adam Green Lough
Victoria Loughlin
Chris Lowe
Rachel Lowery
Sarah Lowis
Ashley Lupson
Bethan Lynch

M

Matthew
Paul M
Andrea Marron
Gemma Marsh
David Marshall
Kayleigh Martell
Amy Martin
Gary Martin
Katherine Martin
Richard Martin
Dean Mason
Stephen Mason
Nik Maynard
Jennifer Mayo
Lucy McAnish
Carly McAuoy
Rosie McCarthy

INDEX

CHILDREN'S BOOK WEEK

INDEX
of contributors

Kirsty McCarvey
Robert McClelland
Helen McDonald
Louise McDowall
Joseph McGovern
Kara McManus
Sophie McShera
Kate Meade
Sarah Melling
Richard Melling
Elizabeth Merrett
Garry Miller
Carli Mitchell
Sophie Moffat
Karen Momarus
Jonathan Moran
Stuart Morris
Ben Mullins
Helen Murphy

Lynn Murray

N

Nicola
Amina Nakhuda
Stephen Neilson
R Nerdsum
Emily-Jayen Newman
Misty Newnham
Adrian Nicholls
Jemma Noble
Katherine Nolan
Liam Norton

O

Daniel O'Connor
Marni O'Mary

JOKE BOOK!

Lauren O'Neill

P

Priva
Nicholas Park
Gary Parker
Charlotte Parkin
Laura Paterson
Liz Pawson
Alice Payne
James Peacock
Gemma Pearson
Victoria Peck
Rebecca Peebles
Ben Pellereau
Kate Pellereau
Christina Phillips
Adam Pinder

Claire Pinder
Laura Price
Ronnie Proudfoot
Scott Proudley
Lyndsey Pursey
Rachel Catherine
Pyke

R

Louise Rathmill
Mary Rayner
Alisha Reece
Priya Melsa Reece
Deborah Rees
Donna Rees
Lauren Rees
Rebecca Rees
Sarah Jane Rees

CHILDREN'S BOOK WEEK

INDEX
of contributors

Abigail Renshaw
Heather Reynolds
John Rice
Andrew Robinson
Anna Robinson
Louise Robinson
Tony Robinson
Sophie Rogers
Katherine Rully
Gemma Ruston
Rachel Rutherford
Catherine Rutter
Patrick Ryan

S

Stuart
Sarah de Sainte

Croix
Dominic Satier
Lee Saunders
Emma Savage
Michael Sayer
Angela Scaccia
Marc Scelecchia
Natalie Scott
Robert Seale
Jodie Selleck
Hayley Sexton
Rebecca Seyburn
Natalie Shaher
Carly Shave
Helen Shaw
Jeremy Shaw
Kerry Shaw
Siobhan Sherwin
Simon Shields

JOKE BOOK!

Trudi Shore
George Smith
Helen Smith
Jemma Smith
Liam Smith
Rachel Soloman
Gemma Staines
Harriet Strachan
Brian Stone
Emma Stoneman
Phillip Stoneman
Bob Swindells

T

Thomas
Christina Tackson
Melissa Takimogh
Luke Taylor

Amy Thomas
Jake Thomas
Alison Thomas
Matthew Thomas
Hannah Thomason
Jake Thorpe
Rachel Thurwell
Rachel Tindall
Rebecca Tinker
Claire Toffle
Kate Tomlinson
Stacey Toporowski
Lindsay Tottle
Lee Townsend
Gemma Tozer
Drew Travers
Gary Trench
Fiona Tullo
Donna Turnbull
Lee Turvey

123

INDEX

of contributors

Thomas Twelvetree

U

Charlie Upton
Jennifer Urwin
Katrina Urwin

V

Amy Vallis
Karl Venus
Sarah Jayne Vernon

W

Wesley
Amanda W
Chloe Waghorn

Jennifer Walker
Heidi Wall
Jamie Wallace
James Ward
Natalie Ward
Richard Waring
Leah Warzynski
Wayne Wass
Amanda Watson
Jade Watson
Sophie Weaver
Chemrse Webster
Emma West
Rachel West
Martin Wheeldon
Nicky White
Lois Whittingham
Christopher Wilkins
Paul Wilkins

JOKE BOOK!

Alex Wilkinson
Rachel Williams
Charlotte Williamson
Helen Williamson
Jacqueline Wilson
Sarah Wilson
Nicola Winterbottom
John Withey
Steven Wright

Y

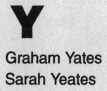

Graham Yates
Sarah Yeates

Z

Zara

CHILDREN'S BOOK WEEK

P.S.

Knock, knock
Who's there?
Thistle
Thistle who?
Thistle'll be the last joke in the book!

Knock Knock